I wish nothing but the good.
Therefore, everyone who does not agree with
me is a traitor and a scoundrel.

King George III

This book is for Balinda and Felix in thanks for a great year together in Brooklyn.

Photographs © 2009: akg-Images, London: 113 (James Gillray), 18 (Thomas Albrecht Pingeling), 10, 94 bottom (Allan Ramsay/Sotheby's); Alamy Images/The Print Collector: 99 top; Art Resource, NY: 99 center (Guildhall Art Gallery, London/HIP), 40 (William Hogarth/Guildhall Art Gallery, London/HIP), 70 (Ann Ronan Picture Library, London/HIP); Bridgeman Art Library International Ltd., London/New York: 87 (Alonzo Chappel/Ken Welsh/Private Collection), 39 (Gerald Coke Handel Collection, Foundling Museum, London), 81 (Emanuel Gottlieb Leutze/Ken Welsh/Private Collection), 42 (Nathaniel Dance Holland/The Hermitage, St. Petersburg), 97 top (Massachusetts Historical Society, Boston), 95 bottom (Museum of London, UK), 98 bottom, 106 (John Nixon/Victoria Art Gallery, Bath and North East Somerset Council), 35, 96 bottom (Ken Welsh/Private Collection), 23, 94 center (Richard Wilson/Yale Center for British Art, Paul Mellon Collection); Corbis Images: 32, 33, 95 top, 96 center, 96 top, 110 (Bettmann), 97 center bottom (Sara Paxton Ball Dadson/Bettmann), 64, 65 (Paul Revere/Bettmann); Getty Images: 115 (Watty Cox's Magazine/Hulton Archive), 45, 98 center (William Gillray/Rischgitz), 93 (Henry Guttmann), 17, 68, 94 top, 99 bottom, 119 (Hulton Archive), 83 (Popperfoto), 29 (Allan Ramsey/Hulton Archive); Superstock, Inc./Image Asset Management Ltd.: 20; The Art Archive/Picture Desk/Culver Pictures: 62, 98 top, 103; The Granger Collection, New York: 53 (P.F. Rothermel), 57 (John Trumbull), 47, 54, 74, 75, 88, 91, 95 center, 97 center top, 97 bottom.

Illustrations by XNR Productions, Inc.: 4, 5, 8, 9
Cover art, page 8 inset by Mark Summers
Chapter art by Raphael Montoliu

Library of Congress Cataloging-in-Publication Data
Brooks, Philip, 1963-
King George III : America's enemy / Philip Brooks.
p. cm. — (A wicked history)
Includes bibliographical references and index.
ISBN-13: 978-0-531-21803-7 (lib. bdg.) 978-0-531-20739-0 (pbk.)
ISBN-10: 0-531-21803-1 (lib. bdg.) 0-531-20739-0 (pbk.)
1. George III, King of Great Britain, 1738-1820—Juvenile literature.
2. Great Britain—History—George III, 1760-1820—Juvenile literature.
3. Great Britain—Kings and rulers—Biography—Juvenile literature. 4.
United States—History—Revolution, 1775-1783—Juvenile literature. I.
Title.
DA506.A2B76 2009
941.07'3092—dc22
[B]

2008040522

Tod Olson, Series Editor
Marie O'Neill, Art Director
Allicette Torres, Cover Design
SimonSays Design!, Book Design and Production

© 2009 Scholastic Inc.

1 2 3 4 5 6 7 8 9 10 R 16 15 14 13 12 11 10 09   23

A WiCKED HISTORY™

King George III

America's Enemy

PHILIP BROOKS

Franklin Watts®
An Imprint of Scholastic Inc.
New York   Toronto   London   Auckland   Sydney
Mexico City   New Delhi   Hong Kong
Danbury, Connecticut

The World of King George III

The British Empire held colonies on the coasts of North America, the Caribbean, Africa, and Asia. These colonies had made Britain rich, and King George was determined to hold on to them—at any cost.

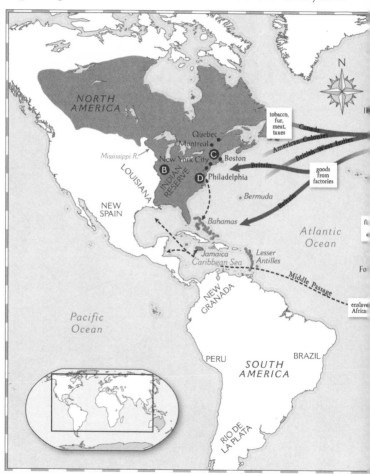

NORTH AMERICA

Quebec
Montreal
Mississippi R.
New York City
B
INDIAN RESERVE
Boston **C**
D Philadelphia

LOUISIANA

NEW SPAIN

Bermuda

Bahamas

Jamaica
Caribbean Sea
Lesser Antilles

NEW GRANADA

Pacific Ocean

PERU

BRAZIL

SOUTH AMERICA

RIO DE LA PLATA

Atlantic Ocean

Middle Passage

tobacco, fur, meat, taxes

Canada

American Colonies

Britain

British West Indies

goods from factories

enslaved Africa

N

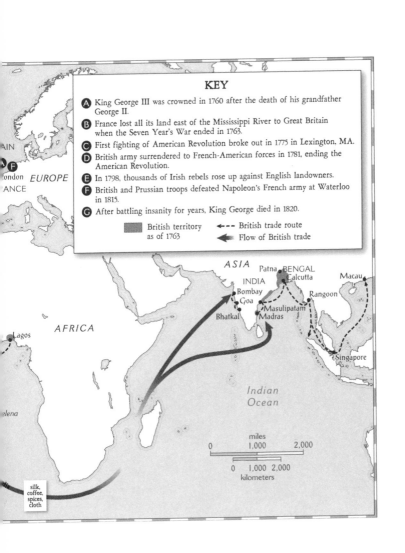

KEY

A King George III was crowned in 1760 after the death of his grandfather George II.

B France lost all its land east of the Mississippi River to Great Britain when the Seven Year's War ended in 1763.

C First fighting of American Revolution broke out in 1775 in Lexington, MA.

D British army surrendered to French-American forces in 1781, ending the American Revolution.

E In 1798, thousands of Irish rebels rose up against English landowners.

F British and Prussian troops defeated Napoleon's French army at Waterloo in 1815.

G After battling insanity for years, King George died in 1820.

     British territory   ◄‑‑ British trade route
     as of 1763   ◄— Flow of British trade

AIN

F

ondon EUROPE
ANCE

ASIA

Patna BENGAL
INDIA   Calcutta   Macau
Bombay   Rangoon
Goa
     Masulipatam
Bhatkal   Madras

Lagos

AFRICA

Singapore

elena

Indian
Ocean

miles
0   1,000   2,000

0   1,000   2,000
kilometers

silk,
coffee,
spices,
cloth

TABLE OF CONTENTS

The World of King George III 4

A Wicked Web 8

Introduction 10

PART 1: RISE OF A KING

CHAPTER 1: A King Is Born 16

CHAPTER 2: Next in Line 21

CHAPTER 3: Love and Power 26

CHAPTER 4: World at War 30

CHAPTER 5: Battle Over Bute 36

CHAPTER 6: Life as King 41

PART 2: EMPIRE IN TURMOIL

CHAPTER 7: Rumbles of Rebellion 50

CHAPTER 8: Stamp of Disapproval 56

CHAPTER 9: Blood in Boston 61

CHAPTER 10: George's Favorite Tax 67

CHAPTER 11: War! 73

CHAPTER 12: Across the Delaware 79

CHAPTER 13: "It Is All Over" 86

KING GEORGE III IN PICTURES 94

PART 3: A TROUBLED MIND

    CHAPTER 14: A Brooding King 102
    CHAPTER 15: Revolution Again 111
    CHAPTER 16: Unbearable Grief 116

Wicked? 120

    Timeline of Terror 122

    Glossary 123

    Find Out More 125

    Index 126

    Author's Note and Bibliography 128

A Wicked Web

A look at the allies and opponents of George III.

The Family of George III

**KING GEORGE II AND
QUEEN CAROLINE**
his grandparents

**FREDERICK, PRINCE
OF WALES**
his father

PRINCESS AUGUSTA
his mother

QUEEN CHARLOTTE
his wife

GEORGE, PRINCE OF WALES
eldest son of George III
and Queen Charlotte

GEORGE III

British Generals

**GENERAL
JOHN BURGOYNE**

**LORD
CHARLES CORNWALLIS**

GENERAL THOMAS GAGE

GENERAL WILLIAM HOWE

British Advisers and Politicians

LORD BUTE
mentor and friend

GEORGE GRENVILLE
prime minister of Great Britain
after the Seven Years' War

LORD ROCKINGHAM
prime minister just before
the American Revolution

LORD NORTH
prime minister during the
American Revolution

WILLIAM PITT, THE ELDER
long-time opponent; then appointed
by George as prime minister during
the American Revolution

WILLIAM PITT, THE YOUNGER
prime minister during
George's illnesses

Rebel Leaders

**SAM ADAMS AND
JAMES OTIS**
leaders of the Sons of Liberty
in Boston

**GENERAL GEORGE
WASHINGTON**
commander of the
Continental Army

**JOHN HANCOCK, JOHN DICKINSON,
THOMAS JEFFERSON, JOHN ADAMS**
other opponents

Rival Leader

NAPOLEON BONAPARTE
emperor of France

KING GEORGE III, 1738–1820

KING GEORGE III AWOKE ON THURSDAY, July 4, 1776, and began his daily routine. His habit during these difficult times was to dress, say his daily prayers, and sit down at his desk in London's Buckingham House to read over military reports. He could not deny, after all, that Great Britain was at war.

Across the Atlantic Ocean, American complaints over taxes and the presence of British troops had exploded into an open revolt against the king. Rebels had attacked royal troops in Massachusetts and forced the king's men out of the city of Boston.

Still, George had little doubt that his well-trained, red-coated soldiers would defeat the farmers and tradesmen who had taken up arms against his authority. Soon enough, the rebels would submit to the will of their loving king.

The stakes of the fight were high. America, with its vast forests and rich fisheries, was the most valuable possession in the British Empire. George did not want to go down in history as the king who lost such a treasure.

Yet as George attended to business in London, rebel leaders gathered in Philadelphia to announce that Americans were breaking free of their king. They adopted the Declaration of Independence, a document that would forever change the way the world saw George III.

The Declaration declared George a "tyrant" who was "unfit to be the ruler of a free people." He had governed and taxed Americans against their will. What's more, the rebel leaders wrote, "He has plundered our seas, ravaged our coasts, burnt our towns, and destroyed the lives of our people."

News of the declaration would take weeks to reach England. Americans learned about it much sooner, as horsemen took off in all directions to spread the word.

Celebrations broke out as the messengers rode from town to town. People lit bonfires in town squares, where angry speeches rallied raucous crowds. Rebels hung straw likenesses of King George from trees and burned them. Paintings of the king were buried in mock funerals. Back in Philadelphia, a rowdy mob pulled a bronze statue of George off its pedestal. They carried the statue to a foundry, where it was melted down to make musket balls for rebel soldiers.

When the news reached King George, the message was clear: The Americans were willing to fight and die for their cause.

George remained equally committed to his. As king, he had sworn an oath to uphold Great Britain's honor. It was his duty—to the country and to God—to defeat these ungrateful traitors. And he vowed to be victorious, no matter the cost.

Rise of a King

CHAPTER 1

A King Is Born

GEORGE ARRIVES EARLY
and begins to be groomed
for the throne.

ON JUNE 3, 1738, PRINCESS AUGUSTA FELT a sharp pain while strolling in the palace gardens. She was only seven months pregnant, so the pains of childbirth should have been several weeks away. But the next morning, she gave birth to a baby boy.

The child was baptized George William Frederick in a simple ceremony. The early birth had left him terribly frail, and doctors worried he might not survive. But a wet nurse named Mary Smith took charge of George's care. She fed him day and night for weeks until he grew strong. She saved the life of a future king.

As soon as he was old enough to understand, George learned that his grandfather ruled the mighty British Empire as King George II. The boy's own father, Frederick, stood next in line for the throne. When Frederick died, young George would rule the most powerful nation on earth.

George's parents wasted no time grooming their son to be king. They encouraged their children to study

GEORGE'S PARENTS, AUGUSTA AND FREDERICK, the princess and prince of Wales. Frederick thought his father, King George II, had dishonored the British crown. Frederick raised young George to be a more pious, patriotic king.

subjects ranging from art and music to science and agriculture. George showed some taste for music and architecture, but little interest in other subjects. Still, he and his siblings spent much of their time with tutors and almost none with friends.

GEORGE III'S GRANDFATHER, King George II, was shockingly loyal to Hanover, a German state that was one of Britain's enemies.

After all, children who held the future of Britain in their hands had to be protected from bad influences.

Nothing protected George from the influence of his own family, however. George's father and grandfather hated each other and did little to hide the fact. King George II came from Hanover (part of present-day Germany), and he insisted that his home country outclassed England in every way. Hanoverians were more intelligent and polite; the soldiers were braver; even the food was tastier. Needless to say, the king's attitude made his British subjects distrust him.

It also made Frederick furious. Frederick thought his father was unpatriotic and corrupt. George II responded by calling his son "the greatest ass, the greatest liar . . . and the greatest beast in the whole world." The year before young George's birth, the king banished Frederick from the royal court.

Frustrated by his banishment, Frederick bitterly claimed that his father was a threat to the glory of Great Britain. He urged young George to be a patriotic and pious king when the time came. Frederick wanted his son to restore the honor that George II had taken from the crown.

As he grew from a shy, very religious boy into a tall, handsome young man, young George felt the weight of his father's expectations. He prayed for the strength to make his father proud. But he had a quiet nature, and public speaking made him nervous. Secretly, he worried he would never make a strong and glorious king.

COLONIZING THE WORLD

BY THE TIME OF GEORGE'S BIRTH, EUROPEANS had been spreading out around the globe for more than two centuries. Explorers and soldiers had blazed trails for settlers throughout the Americas, India, and the Pacific.

The rulers of Europe considered their far-flung settlements to be vital to their security and their economies. Colonies in America and India provided Great Britain with timber, dried fish, tobacco, flour, tea, and spices. And the colonists provided a market for England's textiles and other manufactured goods.

British kings vied with their rivals in Spain, Portugal, France, and Holland for control of the colonies. At times, the struggle led to war. Eventually, the native inhabitants or the colonists themselves began to demand control of their lands.

BRITISH CARGO ships in India.

CHAPTER 2

Next in Line

George loses a father
AND GAINS A MENTOR.

IN 1751, FREDERICK DIED SUDDENLY FROM a lung ailment, leaving his 12-year-old son without a father. George explained the effect of the loss: "I feel something here in my chest," he told his tutor, "just as I did when I saw two workers fall from a scaffold."

George's grandfather, however, seemed untroubled by Frederick's death. King George II was playing cards when a messenger gave him the news. He is said to have told one of his fellow players: "I lost my eldest son. But I am glad of it."

The king soon paid a visit to George's grieving mother, Augusta. George II had never liked the princess, but he held her hand and reportedly even cried a bit. He also spent time with young George and found him to be a "tolerable" boy. The king then promptly fired George's tutors and hand-picked their replacements.

Meanwhile, George drifted lazily through his studies. His tutors agreed that he seemed reasonably intelligent but lacked motivation. He had, however, inherited his grandfather's enthusiasm for criticizing others. One tutor said the prince liked to "compare his own morals with those around him and find them lacking."

As George grew up, he became more and more suspicious of outsiders. Every day seemed to bring new visitors hoping for a favor from their future king. George needed a true friend, a teacher he could trust— and his mother knew just the man.

Lord Bute, an elegant Scottish aristocrat, had been a close friend of George's father. He was somewhat famous for having the "handsomest legs" in London.

YOUNG GEORGE SITS with his brother Edward and a tutor. George had four brothers and four sisters.

After Frederick's death, he spent a lot of time with George's mother. Rumor had it that the two were having an affair, although they denied it.

In 1756, Augusta convinced the king to appoint Bute as George's tutor. George was thrilled. The English people were not. Journalists and politicians distrusted Bute because of his Scottish origins. It had been only five decades since England and Scotland merged to form the Kingdom of Great Britain. Many English still thought of the Scots as foreigners, and they didn't want a foreigner influencing their future king.

In fact, Lord Bute did have a strong influence on George. The two grew very close, and they often discussed what sort of king George should be. Bute had no shortage of strong opinions.

Bute reserved his sternest judgments for a political party called the Whigs, which he hated. For four decades, the Whigs had held a strong grip on the British government. They had a majority in Parliament, the British legislature. They also held many of the powerful positions in the king's ministry, or cabinet.

In general, the Whigs wanted to limit the king's power—a process that had been happening slowly for many years. English kings had always needed the support of the nobility to enforce laws and collect taxes. For more than five centuries, nobles from around the country had gathered in parliaments or councils to approve the king's demands. But during the past 100 years, Parliament had grown much stronger. In 1689, the English Bill of Rights gave some of the kingdom's subjects the right to elect representatives to Parliament. Those representatives had the right to approve taxes and military drafts.

Bute and other monarchists accepted the need to work with Parliament, but they wanted to reserve as much power as possible for the king. They claimed that only the king held Britain's best interests at heart. In their eyes, the Whigs only wanted power for themselves and would stop at nothing to hang onto it. Whig ministers, the monarchists charged, took money in exchange for political favors and gave important jobs to their friends.

Bute urged George to stand above the corruption and restore honor to the government. In practice, that meant fighting the Whigs for control of the country. With Bute at his side, George vowed that he would do his best to turn Britain into a virtuous land. Again and again, he pledged to do everything in his power to be worthy of his "dearest friend's" confidence.

Chapter 3

Love and Power

Ready or not,
Prince George
BECOMES KING.

In the winter of 1759, when George was 21 years old, he fell in love with the most beautiful girl he had ever seen. He hoped to ask Lady Sarah Lennox to marry him. He revealed his plans to Lord Bute and begged for advice. Would Lady Lennox make a suitable queen?

Lord Bute warned him not to marry. Lady Lennox was the sister-in-law of a powerful Whig minister who would be a political rival once George became king.

George ended the romance. He moped for several months, but he knew Bute was right. "I am born for the happiness and misery of a great nation," he wrote to Bute. "Consequently, [I] must often act contrary to my passion."

During the following spring and summer, George spent hours on horseback, hoping to take his mind off Lady Lennox. One autumn morning, he and a group of neighbors were riding through the countryside surrounding his mother's estate. A messenger galloped toward the riding party. He carried a message for George.

George tore open the note. His heart began to race. His aging grandfather had suffered an accident and lay close to death. George excused himself without revealing anything to his friends. He rushed home as fast as he could ride.

When George arrived, Augusta told him that his grandfather had died. The date was October 25, 1760. At the age of 22, George was about to be crowned king of Great Britain.

George had spent his entire life preparing for this moment. Now, he was terrified. He ordered everyone in the household to keep the king's death a secret until further notice. Then he jumped into a carriage and hurried to Lord Bute's estate. He admitted to Bute that he wanted to "hide himself away in a cavern."

That afternoon, George and Lord Bute called an emergency meeting of the Privy Council. The council included the king's cabinet ministers, the most powerful men in Britain. One by one, their splendid coaches arrived at George's mother's London home.

Formal arrangements were made for George to be named king. The privy counselors noticed that the king listened only to Bute's advice as questions arose. Many believed the nervous young king and his Scottish babysitter would need to be taught who was in charge.

For their part, Bute and George viewed the council with scorn. After all, the counselors were politicians, corrupt and immoral. According to George, the worst of them all was William Pitt, his grandfather's secretary of state and the leader of the Whigs. Pitt was already bracing for the first of many battles with the new king of Britain.

LORD BUTE, ADVISER AND FRIEND to King George. Many British politicians distrusted him because of his Scottish origins.

CHAPTER 4

World at War

In his first year as king, GEORGE HAS A RIVAL TO BATTLE and an empire to save.

THE 22-YEAR-OLD KING HAD GOOD reason to be nervous about his new job. A world war had engulfed the globe. And Great Britain, with George's bitter opponent William Pitt directing its war effort, stood right in the middle of it.

When George took the throne, the major powers of Europe were four years into what would later be called the Seven Years' War. For the first time in history, a military conflict had spread to five continents. The fighting ranged from Europe to North America, the Caribbean, India, the Philippines, and the east coast of Africa. Nearly 200,000 people were dying in battle every year.

The war had started in 1756 as a struggle for territory between Austria and the expanding kingdom of Prussia. France, Russia, Sweden, and Saxony joined forces with Austria. George's grandfather entered the war on Prussia's side, but his main target was England's age-old enemy, France.

As secretary of state, Pitt directed Great Britain's armies and foreign affairs. In 1757, during a session of Parliament, he stood and declared: "I know that I can save this country and that no one else can!"

Over the next few years, he seemed to prove himself right. At Pitt's urging, Britain sent tens of thousands of troops to North America, where British and French colonists battled for control of the Ohio River Valley. The British won a big victory there and then invaded French territory in Canada. By the end of 1761, thanks to William Pitt, Britain controlled nearly all of eastern North America.

At home in Europe, the military situation looked bad for a time. British troops tried three times to land on French shores. Each time, they suffered an embarrassing defeat. French forces began to gather along the northern coast of France, ready to cross the English Channel and invade Britain. In 1759, the powerful British navy saved

the day, nearly destroying the entire French fleet in two big battles.

Despite the victories, King George and Lord Bute hated the Seven Years' War. George sincerely felt that the bloodshed was a sin in the eyes of God. Besides, fighting a world war had nearly bankrupted the country. Now that Britain was slowly winning the war with France, George and Bute hoped to cut a deal to end the fighting.

Late in 1761, Lord Bute met with French envoys. As he and George had hoped, the French were tired of fighting. The envoys offered to give up claims to India and parts of North America in exchange for peace. Lord Bute excitedly announced the offer in a meeting of the king's cabinet.

FRENCH AND BRITISH soldiers clash on a battlefield in Canada during the Seven Years' War. During this war, France lost much of its land in North America to Great Britain. The victory made William Pitt a hero in England.

Pitt, hero of the British war effort, urged the cabinet to turn down the offer. There would be no lasting peace, he insisted, until France had been destroyed. Pitt claimed that Spain had signed a secret agreement with France to join forces against Britain. Instead of making peace with France, he said, Britain should declare war against Spain.

Pitt's warmongering enraged George. The king distrusted all politicians. He soon grew to hate Pitt. The Whig leader, he felt, had publicly upstaged him. Privately, Pitt was bullying and disrespectful in their meetings. George wrote to Bute, complaining bitterly that he felt like Pitt's servant and prisoner: "I cannot help telling [you,] my Dearest Friend, that my honor is here at stake."

George and Bute pressed their case in the cabinet— and won the showdown. Most of the ministers deserted Pitt and voted to negotiate with France for peace. Stripped of his support, Pitt resigned in October 1761.

WILLIAM PITT directed Britain's victories in the Seven Years' War. He was a national hero, but King George despised him.

The English people were shocked to lose their war hero. Politician and journalist Horace Walpole described the nation as "thunderstruck, alarmed, and indignant." He added: "It is difficult to say which exulted most on the occasion, France, Spain, or Lord Bute."

With Pitt gone, Bute took over his responsibilities. George congratulated Bute for his strong stand against "Mr. Pitt's black scheme." He believed his loyal subjects would soon see that Pitt's resignation was for the best.

CHAPTER 5

Battle Over Bute

George's friend finds peace overseas—
AND RESENTMENT AT HOME.

A FEW WEEKS AFTER PITT'S RESIGNATION,
George's subjects got a chance to make their voices
heard. In keeping with tradition, a huge party broke
out across London on Lord Mayor's Day—the day
the city's mayor takes office. The streets filled with
revelers, many of whom had been drinking ale all day
long. The day ended with a banquet for the nation's
leaders at Guildhall, home of the city government.
Crowds lined the streets leading to the hall to cheer
or jeer each dignitary's arrival.

One by one, the carriages pulled up for the banquet. The people easily recognized Pitt's carriage. It had a raised leather support for his aching foot, which was hobbled by a painful blood disease known as gout. When Pitt rolled up to Guildhall, the crowd cheered wildly. Well-wishers hung on doors of his carriage and even kissed his horses.

The king's heavy, gold-encrusted coach arrived shortly after. It drew polite silence from the crowd. Then another carriage rolled up, and someone shouted, "By God, this is Bute! Be damned to him!" The crowd vented its anger at the "foreigner" by pelting his carriage with mud. "No Scotch rogues!" the people cried.

Bute had hired a squad of professional boxers to act as bodyguards. But the mob was too angry to be held back. Mounted police had to join the scuffle and rescue the terrified Bute before his coach was overturned.

Pitt was cheered again as he limped through the huge doors of Guildhall. Politicians praised his achievements in speech after speech. The king and

Lord Bute were largely ignored, which made George furious. The day after the celebration, he wrote to Bute: "This is, I believe, the wickedest age that ever was seen."

To make matters worse, peace talks with France soon broke down. In January 1762, Britain was forced into war with Spain, just as Pitt had predicted.

George was heartbroken. He begged Bute to take the job of prime minister and see the war through to its end. Bute dreaded the thought of taking such a public position, but he gave in to the king's pleas.

Near the end of 1762, Bute helped negotiate the Treaty of Paris, ending the Seven Years' War. Russia had abruptly pulled out of its alliance with France, and the French were desperate to stop fighting. Bute was able to get his way in the treaty negotiations. Spain gave up Florida to the British. France gave up Canada, the Ohio River Valley, and important rights in India. Despite Pitt's objections, the treaty was overwhelmingly approved by Parliament.

CELEBRATIONS IN LONDON marked the end of the Seven Years' War. The victory had made Britain a great world power.

"*Now* my son is king of England!" crowed Augusta after the victory.

Feeling his work was done, Bute promptly resigned.

George had a lot to be proud of after his first two years as king. He had humbled Pitt, the leader of the Whigs, and won the war at the same time. Britain's navy had firmly established its control of the seas. Its ground forces had pushed the French out of North America. The British Empire was now the most powerful in the world. And at the age of 24, King George III ruled it all.

DANGER IN THE STREETS

IT'S NO WONDER THAT UNPOPULAR OFFICIALS like Bute lived in fear of mob violence. London in George's time was a wild place. Horse manure and human waste polluted the streets. Men carried clubs for self-protection.

London's police had trouble keeping crime under control. But when a criminal was caught, punishment was swift and cruel. A thief could get the death penalty for stealing five shillings from a shop. Hangings often took place in public before eager audiences.

If no hangings were scheduled, Londoners had other blood sports to choose from. Gamblers bet on cockfights, in which roosters battled to the death with razors attached to their feet. Bear-baiting also drew crowds, who cheered while dogs were unleashed to attack a chained bear.

LONDON GAMBLERS at a cockfight.

CHAPTER 6

Life as King

George attends to his family
AND HIS SUBJECTS.

WITH THE BRITISH EMPIRE AT PEACE
for the first time in nine years, George was able to attend
to private business. During his two years on the throne,
he had acquired a small but rapidly growing family.

Soon after George was crowned, Princess Augusta
and Lord Bute had conducted an exhaustive search for
an appropriate queen. They consulted a long list of
Europe's princesses to find someone who came from a
suitable family. They eventually chose a young German
princess with a spotless reputation. Details of her

family's history were given to the Privy Council, and it quickly approved the marriage. The 17-year-old Duchess Sophia Charlotte sailed to England, memorizing a few English sentences along the way. She and George married on September 8, 1761, just days after they met.

DUCHESS SOPHIA CHARLOTTE was chosen to be George's wife on the condition that she promise to keep out of politics. She and George became very close.

George found his bride to be much less beautiful than Lady Lennox, but "quite agreeable." The two soon grew affectionate with each other. Charlotte playfully asked George to get rid of the powdered wig worn by many men of the time. She suggested he let his shiny chestnut-colored hair grow out, and he happily granted her wish. For his part, George came to describe his queen as "a true friend." By the end of 1763, Charlotte had already given birth to two royal heirs, George and Frederick. (She would have 15 children in all over the next 20 years.)

Comfortable in his new roles as husband and father, George turned to the duties of a peacetime king. He proved to be diligent and devoted to his work. He rose early each day, shaved, and said his prayers. He personally lit the fire in his study and got straight to work. Through the years he would often remind his children that the early morning hours were the most productive. He believed that work—and plenty of it—was good for the soul and mind. "If the mind be not constantly in the habit of serious employment it will lose its energy," he wrote.

George answered countless letters, examined requests for money or jobs, and approved appointments to government posts. Military promotions also had to be reviewed and signed.

George became famous for his attention to detail and his memory. As he followed the events of the Seven Years' War, he learned the name of every ship in the British navy. He knew the location and the commander of each army battalion. It was often said that the king would have gladly managed the daily affairs of each and every one of his subjects.

After a morning of paperwork, the king usually took a ride on horseback. He believed it was important to be physically active and vigorous. After riding, he ate a simple breakfast and returned to his desk.

George loved to hunt and to visit the farms surrounding his country palaces. He enjoyed checking on local livestock, particularly pigs. His habit of stopping to chat with his subjects about their crops and herds eventually earned him the nickname "Farmer George." It wasn't always used with affection.

Though he was well-educated and cultured, George liked to think of himself as a simple man with simple

IN THIS POLITICAL CARTOON, George and Charlotte
are shown visiting a farmer. The king was mocked for his
fascination with country life.

virtues. His Protestant faith was important to him, and he wanted its strict morals to govern the lives of his subjects as well. To this end, he issued a royal proclamation for the "Encouragement of Piety and Virtue." The new law required British subjects to attend church every week. It also outlawed dancing on Sundays, raised taxes on beer, and promised stricter penalties for gambling. The proclamation made the king even more unpopular with the English people.

But King George III soon learned that his subjects at home were the least of his worries. As a result of the Seven Years' War, he now had new territories in North America to defend and new subjects to govern. George had never visited America and had no interest in doing so. He could hardly imagine such a vast and wild land. Nevertheless, the distant colonies began to demand his attention.

No Coughing Allowed!

AS A FATHER, GEORGE LOVED TO GET ON THE
floor and play with his brood of children. As king, however,
he had no patience for amusements.

The king and queen were known for holding all
visitors to a strict code of behavior. Once, the queen was
asked whether a pregnant lady-in-waiting could be allowed
to sit. Queen Charlotte sniffed and denied permission. One
did not sit in the presence of royalty.

Fanny Burney, a writer who spent time in George's
court wrote, "In the first place you must not cough. If
you find a tickling in your throat, you must arrest it from
making any sound." She went on, jokingly: "If by chance
a hat pin runs into your
head, you must not take
it out. If the pain is very
great, you must bear it
without wincing."

THE ROYAL FAMILY
at a private concert in
Buckingham House.

PART 2

Empire in Turmoil

CHAPTER 7

Rumbles of Rebellion

George makes the Americans
pay their way and is
ACCUSED OF TYRANNY.

IN 1763, GEORGE DECIDED HE HAD TO
lower the cost of defending the American colonists.
The Ottawa chief Pontiac had led attacks on British
forts in the Great Lakes region, and British troops
were once again at war. To keep frontier conflicts
at bay, the king ordered settlers to stay east of the
Appalachian Mountains. This border was called the

Proclamation Line of 1763. (See map on page 85 to see the 13 original colonies and this new border.)

To George, and to most Members of Parliament, this seemed like a practical idea. To the colonists, it felt like tyranny. Many of them had risked their lives to seize the Ohio River Valley from the French and their Native American allies. Now the king wanted them to abandon it. Letters and petitions arrived on George's desk, demanding a change in the law.

Instead of backing down, the British decided to make the colonists pay for their own protection. In the spring of 1764, the king's prime minister, George Grenville, got Parliament to pass a law known as the Sugar Act. The act required the Americans to pay a tax on the molasses they imported from the Caribbean. Revenues from the tax would help pay for the British soldiers stationed in the colonies. More British warships were sent to North America with instructions to arrest anyone who tried to smuggle in untaxed molasses.

As fresh British soldiers arrived in Boston, New York, and Virginia to enforce the tax laws, a small band of colonists began to organize resistance. In Boston, James Otis and Samuel Adams led a protest against the Sugar Act. They convinced local merchants to boycott imported British goods. The Americans had no representatives in the British Parliament, Adams pointed out. Therefore, Parliament had no right to tax the Americans. Before long, "No taxation without representation!" became the rallying cry for a growing protest in the colonies.

At first, King George and Prime Minister Grenville ignored Adams and Otis and pressed for new taxes. In March 1765, Grenville pushed the Stamp Act through Parliament. The law required Americans to pay for an official seal—or stamp—that would be attached to all legal documents, newspapers, almanacs, and playing cards.

In Virginia, a young lawyer named Patrick Henry joined the protest. Henry made a bold speech before Virginia's legislature, in which he called King George

PATRICK HENRY CONDEMNS King George in a famous 1765 speech before the Virginia legislature. Henry argued that George was violating the colonists' rights as British subjects by taxing them without giving them a say in their own government.

a bully and a tyrant. He compared George to the Roman emperor Julius Caesar and to the English king Charles I, both of whom were killed for abusing their power. "May George III profit from their example!" Henry declared.

In the summer of 1765, George could have spent his time trying to calm his angry American subjects. Instead, he squabbled with his prime minister. The king and Grenville were constantly struggling over petty issues. Grenville tried to control appointments to jobs as insignificant as Court Painter. Worst of all, he bored the king to tears with endless reports and speeches. "When he has wearied me for two hours, he looks at his

PRIME MINISTER GRENVILLE agreed with King George that the Americans should be taxed. But the two men argued about everything else.

watch to see if he may not tire me for an hour more," George complained.

In July, George finally got rid of Grenville, but the victory was costly. The Whigs refused to cooperate with George unless he forced the meddling Lord Bute to step aside. Eventually, George gave in and distanced himself from his "Dearest Friend." Bute left London, understanding that he was no longer welcome in the king's presence.

The struggle left George angry and brooding for weeks. He developed an illness his physician called "a severe cold." He slept only two hours a night and felt anxious all the time. Rumors that the king was gravely ill spread from Parliament to the newspapers.

"I am not ill," George protested to his family and royal physicians. "Just very, very nervous."

CHAPTER 8

Stamp of Disapproval

Riots in the streets
of Boston FORCE THE KING
TO BACK DOWN.

AS THE SUMMER OF 1765 NEARED ITS END, George had good reason to be nervous. In the colonies, the Stamp Act had sparked a growing protest movement. Secret "Sons of Liberty" groups formed in many towns to organize resistance to the tax. The Boston group, led by Adams and Otis, acted first.

AMERICAN COLONISTS HARASS two British tax collectors. The colonists were enraged by the Stamp Act, which required them to pay taxes on all legal documents, newspapers, and other printed items.

One hot August day, an angry mob of Bostonians made a likeness of the royal stamp commissioner by stuffing some clothes with straw. They strung the straw dummy from a tree in an act of protest known as "hanging in effigy." Leaving the dummy swinging in the breeze, the mob surged through the streets to the tax collector's office, where they smashed windows and pounded holes in the walls. Next they swarmed toward the stately home of the stamp commissioner. The commissioner's terrified family and servants cowered in a corner as the mob smashed windows. The rioters burst inside and threw furniture and family portraits into the street. A few days later, another mob ransacked the home of the colony's lieutenant governor.

By November 1765, when the Stamp Act was supposed to take effect, every stamp commissioner in America had quit his job for fear of similar treatment.

Parliament met to consider how to handle the Americans, and the debate returned George's old enemy to center stage. William Pitt had been ill with gout when the Stamp Act was passed. He now creaked painfully to his feet and argued that the law was unjust; the Americans should not be taxed without representation in Parliament. If the king wanted to keep the Americans in the empire, Pitt insisted, he needed to compromise.

Pitt's argument won a lot of support in Parliament. Even the members who thought the tax was fair feared that collecting it had become impossible. Would the crown have to send more troops? Where would they come from, and how would they be paid?

Pitt and the new prime minister, Lord Rockingham, convinced George that there was only one thing to do: Repeal the Stamp Act. With the king's support, Parliament did just that in March 1766. Thankful Americans cheered George and Pitt. New Yorkers even erected a statue in the king's honor.

But the battle did not end with the repeal of the Stamp Act. George hated any appearance of weakness. With his support, Parliament passed the Declaratory

Act, announcing that Britain had the right to make laws governing the colonies "in all cases whatsoever."

When George fully recovered his health in 1766, he celebrated by firing Rockingham, whom he considered weak. Now the king had to find a new prime minister, and he turned to William Pitt. George had privately called Pitt a "snake in the grass." But Pitt was smart and tough. He was trusted by the American rebel leaders and could help George deal with them.

In the summer of 1766, Pitt agreed to return as prime minister. Then he promptly retired to the resort town of Bath to nurse his gout. In his absence, the government got almost nothing done, prompting an opposition leader to comment, "[Pitt] is at Bath and consequently the King's Administration has also got the gout and hobbles terribly."

CHAPTER 9

Blood in Boston

THE MOB PICKS A FIGHT
with the king's soldiers.

WHILE PITT LAY IN BED AT BATH, KING George and Parliament tried once more to raise money from the Americans. The Townshend Acts, passed in November 1767, placed new taxes on certain household goods imported into the country. Among the items taxed were paper, glass, and tea. To enforce the law, British officials in America redoubled their efforts to catch smugglers. They boarded the ships of

American merchants and tore through the cargo holds looking for taxable goods.

In the summer of 1768, British soldiers in Boston Harbor seized a cargo ship owned by an American merchant named John Hancock. Angry mobs rioted in the streets in protest. One group stormed the Customs House and demanded the release of Hancock's ship. British officials had no choice but to let the vessel go.

At this point, George could have called for negotiations with rebel leaders. But the violence

PAUL REVERE MADE this engraving of British warships entering Boston Harbor. The Royal Navy was patrolling the American coastline to seize merchant ships carrying untaxed cargo.

seemed inexcusable to him. So instead of looking for compromises, he called on the British army.

In October, General Thomas Gage sent two regiments of British soldiers from Canada to Boston to stamp out protests and enforce the tax laws. For the next year and a half, the city hung on the brink of violence. When the red-coated soldiers patrolled the streets, colonists gathered in doorways to yell insults at them. Week after week, tempers grew shorter and conflicts more frequent.

Finally, on the night of March 5, 1770, the tension erupted into violence. It began when a wig maker's apprentice taunted a British officer for failing to pay a bill to his master. Another soldier joined the argument and eventually hit the apprentice with his musket. A crowd gathered to throw snowballs at the soldier. Church bells rang around the city as word of the confrontation spread.

More British soldiers arrived, and within hours they faced a jeering crowd of 300 or 400 on the steps of the Customs House. The frightened soldiers formed a semicircle, bayonets at the ready. Suddenly, a man hit one of the soldiers with a club. The soldier struggled to his feet and fired his musket into the crowd. "Damn you, fire!" he shouted to his fellow soldiers. They did.

When the smoke cleared, 11 Bostonians lay wounded. Within two weeks, five of them were dead and pamphlets had begun to circulate announcing the "bloody massacre" in Boston.

By now it was clear to the king and to Parliament that the rebels had made it impossible to enforce the Townshend Acts. Royal officials in the colonies feared for their lives. Boycotts were putting British merchants out of business. A month after the Boston Massacre, Parliament voted to repeal all taxes except one—the tax on imported tea.

"There must always be one tax to keep up the right [to tax]," George told his ministers. "And as such I approve of the tea duty."

The king consoled himself further by the fact that he finally had a prime minister he liked. In January, he had asked a longtime Member of Parliament, Lord North, to lead the government. George

BRITISH REDCOATS SHOOT American protesters during the notorious Boston Massacre. A month later, Parliament would try to regain the colonists' loyalty by repealing most of the new taxes.

had known North since they were boys. The two men looked so much alike that some people suggested they had to be closely related.

Lord North was extremely effective in Parliament. He was a shrewd politician who had made many important friends in London. During debates he often seemed to be asleep in his seat, only to "wake up" and deliver a wise or witty remark. As prime minister, Lord North managed to convince the Members of Parliament to vote with the king's position on issue after issue.

Many journalists and politicians spoke out against the king gaining so much control over Parliament. But George did not see what the fuss was about. God had made him a righteous king. He wanted only what was best for his subjects. There was no such thing as too much power so long as it was wielded for the glory of Great Britain.

CHAPTER 10

George's Favorite Tax

A TEA PARTY brings the king closer to war.

AS GEORGE STRUGGLED TO CONTROL the rebels in America, he began to act as though he were battling a rebellion under his own roof. By 1773, after just 11 years of marriage, he already had nine kids. George held them all to high standards. They were to pray often and spend much of the day studying.

The king was hardest on his sons. He ordered that the princes be beaten for lying, laziness, or vanity. One of George's daughters later recalled how her brothers were regularly "flogged like dogs with a long whip" by their tutors.

The king worried most about his eldest boy, George, who stood next in line for the throne. King George and his wife were certain that their son showed distinct signs of moral weakness. He ate and drank too much and loved to wear fancy clothes. Queen Charlotte urged

THE FAMILY OF KING GEORGE III. Queen Charlotte and King George had 15 children. He complained about most of them.

her son to "disdain all flattery" and "abhor all vice." It was the prince's duty, she reminded him, to "do justice unto everybody" and display "the highest love, affection, and duty towards the King."

George loved his children deeply. He felt about his sons and daughters much the way he felt about his subjects in America: He believed he was doing what was best for them, no matter how much it pained them. Still, relations between the children and their parents grew understandably chilly.

In America, there was even less warmth to be found. Rather than paying the tea tax, the colonists had begun to smuggle tea leaves in enormous quantities. Patriotic Americans called legally imported tea "the beverage of traitors" and refused to drink the stuff.

On December 16, 1773, a ship called the *Dartmouth* rocked gently in Boston Harbor, its hold full of British tea. Near midnight, a group of rebels disguised as Mohawk Indians boarded the *Dartmouth*, broke open the tea chests with tomahawks, and dumped the tea

BOSTONIANS DRESSED as Native Americans toss British tea into the harbor. After this protest against British taxation, King George was ready to go to war to force his American subjects to submit.

into the harbor. Then they snatched a nearby customs official from his bed and tarred and feathered him. He was badly hurt but survived the ordeal.

The English were outraged when news of the Boston Tea Party reached their shores. One Member of Parliament wanted Boston to be bombarded with cannons. Another told Parliament, "You will never meet with proper obedience to the laws of this country until you have destroyed that nest of locusts." A famous writer named Samuel Johnson called the Americans "a race of convicts." He declared that they should be happy with any treatment "short of hanging."

For George, the Tea Party was the last straw. He did not want to start a war, but he felt that harsh punishment was needed. He had to tame the rebels, or Great Britain would lose respect in Europe. "The die is cast," he wrote. "The colonies must either triumph or submit."

In 1774, the British military swung into action. A Royal Navy fleet sailed to the coast of Boston, blockading the city until the colonists paid for the ruined tea. In May, General Gage arrived to impose martial law on Massachusetts. His orders were to maintain the peace, using force only as a last resort.

George hoped that a firm response in Massachusetts would intimidate the other colonies. Instead it pushed them to the brink of full rebellion. In September 1774, delegates from Massachusetts and 11 other colonies gathered in Philadelphia for the First Continental Congress. They voted to unite to boycott British goods and to protect Massachusetts from a British attack.

The prospect of war got old William Pitt out of his sickbed and back into Parliament. Even now, he commanded great respect as an orator. In obvious pain from his gout, he stood and insisted that the American rebel leaders had right on their side. "I trust it is obvious to your lordships that all attempts to impose servitude upon such men, to establish despotism over such a mighty continental nation, must be in vain, must be fatal," he said. "We shall be forced ultimately to retract. Let us retract while we can, not when we must."

Such talk enraged George. "I wish nothing but the good," he blustered. "Therefore, everyone who does not agree with me is a traitor and a scoundrel."

CHAPTER 11

War!

George's redcoats face
THE REBEL MILITIA.

BY THE END OF 1774, IT LOOKED LIKE King George would have to fight to hold his empire together. In September, General Gage's soldiers seized a stash of gunpowder in Somerville, Massachusetts. The rebels had obviously started preparing for war.

Gage soon learned that the rebels were collecting weapons and ammunition at another armory in Concord, 15 miles from Boston. Late on the night of April 18, 1775, a regiment of 700 British soldiers rowed out of Boston Harbor and headed quietly up the

Charles River. Their mission was to arrest Sam Adams and John Hancock in Lexington, and then move upriver to destroy the armory in Concord. But as the soldiers approached Lexington at dawn, church bells rang out to warn of their arrival. Thanks to Paul Revere and other messengers, the colonists were expecting the British.

Gage's troops marched into Lexington to find 70

rebel militiamen guarding the town green with rifles. The British formed a firing line; the militiamen did the same. Townsfolk gathered to watch the tense standoff.

Suddenly a shot rang out, though no one knew who fired it. Confusion led to panic. The British line opened fire, and 18 Americans were killed or wounded. The survivors scrambled to safety, and the British

THE AMERICAN REVOLUTION begins with the Battle of Lexington. Here, American militiamen try to withstand volleys of musket-shot from a line of British redcoats. But the British had superior firepower, and the Americans were forced to retreat.

continued on their march. After finding the armory at Concord empty, they made their way back to Boston, dodging sniper fire along the way.

The American Revolution had begun.

Word of the skirmishes spread quickly through the colonies. Farmers and craftsmen grabbed their muskets and hurried to Boston. They laid siege to the city from the heights of Bunker Hill and Breed's Hill.

General Gage was determined to snuff out the rebellion before it could spread. On June 17, his men attacked the rebels and pushed them off the heights. The Battle of Bunker Hill counted as a British victory, but it did nothing to crush the rebels' morale. New militiamen poured in from the countryside. General Gage knew he was in for a fight. "These people show a spirit . . . as great as ever people were possessed of," he told his fellow generals.

Two months later, King George got a chance to make peace with the spirited colonists. A letter arrived in London, written and signed by John Dickinson,

Thomas Jefferson, and other rebel leaders. The letter claimed that the rebels wanted to remain loyal to the crown. If George would give them a say in working out fair trade and tax policies, they would lay down their arms. The letter soon became known as the Olive Branch Petition.

There it was, within the king's grasp: a chance to end the war almost before it started. But another letter arrived around the same time, this one written by rebel leader John Adams to a friend. Somehow the letter had fallen into the hands of royal officials, who immediately sent it to the king. In the letter, Adams ridiculed the Olive Branch Petition. War was inevitable, he wrote, and the rebels should not be seeking peace from the king. Instead, they should immediately raise a navy and arrest as many British colonial officials as they could find.

Adams's letter killed any hope for peace. It made the king so angry that he refused to respond to the Olive Branch Petition. Instead he resolved to pursue the war until the rebels were crushed. "May my deluded subjects on the other side of the Atlantic behold their pending destruction with half the horror that I feel on the occasion," he wrote.

But the news from across the Atlantic must have made the king wonder whose destruction was pending. In March 1776, massive cannons appeared on the heights of Boston and forced the British to evacuate the city. Three months later, rebel leaders announced their dramatic Declaration of Independence.

George must have been furious when he read this document. The king of Great Britain a tyrant? His government unjust? The rebels even insisted that people had the right to overthrow their rulers. The king grew more determined than ever to destroy the arrogant rebels before they did real damage to the glory of the British Empire.

CHAPTER 12

Across the Delaware

The "colonial rabble" proves
more than A MATCH
FOR THE BRITISH ARMY.

WITH THE REBEL ARMY GROWING FAST,
King George and his generals had to find a way to
fight a full-blown war 3,500 miles away from home.
Great Britain had about 49,000 soldiers spread across
four continents. Many people felt the king could not
gather enough troops to win a war in America. George
dismissed them as defeatists and traitors.

To the horror of many Englishmen, George hired thousands of foreigners—many of them Germans from the state of Hesse—to fight in America. How dare he send foreign troops to attack his own subjects! George ignored the criticism.

During the fall and winter of 1776, the king was pleased with reports of the war's progress. British troops chased General George Washington and his Continental Army out of New York and into New Jersey. By December, Washington had retreated as far west as Pennsylvania. The exhausted Americans ran short of food and supplies. Washington's 6,000 cold and hungry soldiers camped in the snow by the Delaware River. On the other side, near Trenton, New Jersey, were 1,400 well-equipped Hessians awaiting orders to attack. The king thought he was on the verge of stamping out the uprising.

Then came General Washington's Christmas surprise.

On Christmas night, Washington rallied his men.

He took the soldiers who were healthy enough to fight and led them across the icy Delaware. Washington's men, many of them marching barefoot through the snow, attacked and routed the Hessians.

British General Charles Cornwallis hurried 8,000 of his best soldiers to New Jersey. But the outnumbered

GENERAL WASHINGTON and his men cross the frozen Delaware River to ambush a Hessian army at Trenton, New Jersey. Before this surprise victory, it had seemed that the ragged and starving Continental Army would be forced to surrender.

Americans scored a shocking victory at Princeton. Washington settled in for the winter, and the British had to plan for another year of fighting.

When news of the defeats arrived from across the ocean, George brooded. But he still considered the Continental Army to be nothing more than a "cowardly colonial rabble." It shouldn't take long for the king's men to put them in their place.

In the summer of 1777, the king's commanders in America set out to prove him right. General John Burgoyne led 10,000 men down Lake Champlain from Canada, hoping to cut New England off from the rest of the colonies. General William Howe led 15,000 troops southwest from New York City to seize Philadelphia, the headquarters of the Continental Congress. On September 26, Howe took the rebel capital without firing a shot.

Reports of the victory reached London some weeks later. George raced into the queen's room shouting, "I have beat them! Beat the Americans!"

But the king celebrated too soon. By the time he learned of the fall of Philadelphia, Burgoyne had been surrounded at Saratoga, New York. He was forced to surrender. Howe was barely in better shape than Burgoyne, despite his victory in Philadelphia. He insisted his army was too weak to continue. He wrote

BRITISH GENERAL JOHN BURGOYNE (left) surrenders his sword to General George Washington after Burgoyne's defeat in the Battle of Saratoga.

to London, threatening to resign if he did not receive reinforcements.

At least some people felt that King George did not fully understand the danger of the situation. The day after word of Burgoyne's surrender reached him, George attended a party in his own honor. The king spent the night laughing loudly and drinking toasts to the glory of the British Empire. Several of the king's friends took him aside to warn him that the display was embarrassing.

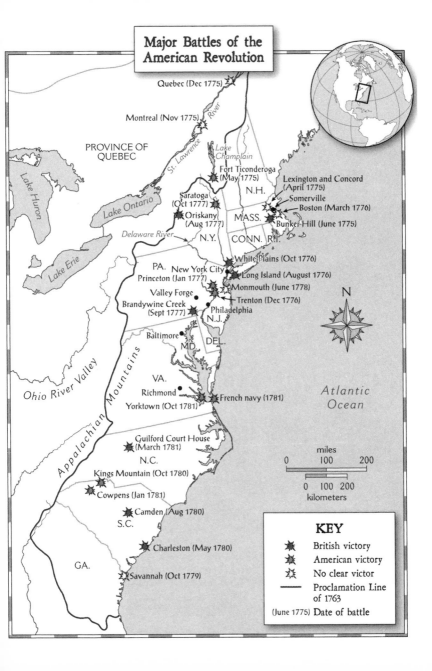

Major Battles of the American Revolution

Quebec (Dec 1775)

Montreal (Nov 1775)

PROVINCE OF QUEBEC

St. Lawrence River

Lake Champlain

Fort Ticonderoga (May 1775)

Lexington and Concord (April 1775)

Saratoga (Oct 1777)

Somerville

N.H.

Boston (March 1776)

Oriskany (Aug 1777)

MASS.

Bunker Hill (June 1775)

Lake Ontario

Lake Huron

Delaware River

N.Y.

CONN. R.I.

White Plains (Oct 1776)

Lake Erie

PA.

New York City

Long Island (August 1776)

Princeton (Jan 1777)

Monmouth (June 1778)

Valley Forge

Trenton (Dec 1776)

Brandywine Creek (Sept 1777)

Philadelphia

N.J.

Baltimore

MD. DEL.

Ohio River Valley

VA.

N

Richmond

French navy (1781)

Atlantic Ocean

Yorktown (Oct 1781)

Appalachian Mountains

Guilford Court House (March 1781)

N.C.

miles

0   100   200

Kings Mountain (Oct 1780)

0   100 200

Cowpens (Jan 1781)

kilometers

Camden (Aug 1780)

S.C.

Charleston (May 1780)

GA.

Savannah (Oct 1779)

KEY

✳ British victory

✳ American victory

✳ No clear victor

— Proclamation Line of 1763

(June 1775) Date of battle

CHAPTER 13

"It Is All Over"

THE REBELLION TRIUMPHS
with the help of England's
old foe, France.

THE BRITISH AND THE AMERICANS SPENT
the winter of 1777 in a stalemate. General Howe's
forces took over expensive homes in Philadelphia
and rested in style. General Washington's army
camped out at Valley Forge, 18 miles outside the
city. Hundreds of American soldiers froze to death
or died of disease. But those who survived trained
hard. The Continental Army emerged from the
winter a professional fighting force.

GENERALS WASHINGTON AND LAFAYETTE at
Valley Forge. Lafayette convinced his king, Louis XVI, to ally
with the Americans—a crushing blow for King George and
the British Empire.

In February, the rebel army got a lift from England's
age-old enemies. The French signed a treaty recognizing
the United States as a new nation. They pledged soldiers,
ships, and money to help defeat Britain.

George tried to remain calm. France's intervention
was an "unhappy event," he admitted. But surely his
redcoats could defeat the combined armies.

Parliament, however, was beginning to lose faith in the war effort. More and more members began to argue that Britain should let America go. In April, William Pitt struggled to his feet in the House of Lords to join the debate. For years he had urged the king to negotiate with the Americans. But he had never wanted

THE DEATH OF WILLIAM PITT. He had helped make Britain the mightiest nation on earth. King George desperately missed his leadership during the fight to keep the American colonies.

to lose the colonies he had fought for during the Seven Years' War. He insisted that Britain must continue the fight. Nearing the end of his speech, he collapsed and never recovered.

King George found himself mourning his old opponent's death. Pitt had wanted peace while George remained committed to war. But the two agreed above all that North America must stay in the British Empire.

With the French in the war, that outcome looked more and more unlikely. The British army reduced its presence in the northern colonies and turned to the south, where George hoped to find Americans who were still loyal to the crown. A few victories in the south, he believed, would inspire these loyalists to join with the British and sweep their rebel countrymen aside.

George got his victories, but the loyalists never materialized. In 1779 and 1780, the British rolled through Georgia and South Carolina. But when the redcoats invaded Virginia, rebels quickly recaptured Georgia and South Carolina. In July 1781, the British general Lord

Cornwallis retreated to Yorktown, Virginia. There, on the coast, he waited for the Royal Navy to transport his army back to New York.

The Royal Navy never arrived.

In September, a combined force of American and French soldiers converged on Yorktown and besieged Cornwallis's army. For ten days, General Washington battered the British with heavy artillery. After taking more than 35,000 shells, Cornwallis decided he could no longer withstand the siege. On October 19, 1781, he surrendered to the Americans.

Word of the massive defeat reached London a month later. Most of Parliament gave up any hope of winning the war. "Oh God!" Lord North said. "It is all over!"

George, on the other hand, refused to accept defeat. He proposed a plan to harass the colonists by land and sea. With a strong effort, he insisted, the British could "keep the rebels harassed, anxious, and poor."

Parliament quickly rejected the king's plan as too expensive and too dangerous. The 22-year-old son of

BRITISH GENERAL CORNWALLIS is shown in this artwork surrendering his army to General Washington after the Siege of Yorktown. In reality, Cornwallis didn't surrender in person; he sent his second-in-command.

William Pitt, William Pitt the Younger, declared the war "wicked, barbarous, cruel, unjust, and diabolical." Even Lord North abandoned the king. George denounced his old friend, declaring him a traitor.

In September 1783, Parliament recognized the United States of America as a free nation. George did not attend the ceremonies or the signing of the treaty.

Despite the king's stubbornness, eight years of war had come to an end. About 20,000 British soldiers had died on the battlefield, along with 8,000 Hessian mercenaries. The failed war cost the British treasury huge amounts of cash and put the kingdom in debt for many years to come.

George did not blame himself for the disaster of the war. "I am innocent of the evils that have occurred," he said. But he did describe himself as "deeply wounded that it should have happened during my reign."

Long after the last shots had been fired, however, George lay awake wondering what he might have done differently to defeat Washington and his "rabble." Once, he had imagined himself a great ruler who would bring glory to the British Empire. Instead, he had become the king who lost America.

THE BRITISH SLAVE TRADE

DURING THE REIGN OF GEORGE III, BRITAIN was the richest nation in the world. And much of that wealth came from the Atlantic slave trade.

English merchants would send ships to the western coast of Africa. There, the ships' captains bought Africans from kidnappers. The ships then sailed across the Atlantic Ocean to sugar plantations in the Caribbean, where 80,000 new slaves were purchased every year to replace those who had died from disease or overwork.

By 1787, most English people wanted to abolish this brutal system. But slave owners in Parliament resisted, and George worried that France would swoop in and seize the profits. Britain finally outlawed the slave trade in 1807, but slavery remained legal in the British colonies until 1838.

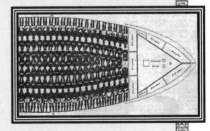

THIS DRAWING of a brutally packed slave ship horrified thousands of Britons.

King George III in Pictures

MEET THE PARENTS
George's parents, Augusta and Frederick. As the oldest son of King George II, Frederick was heir to the British throne. However, he died before George II did. That put young George next in line.

BAD GRADES
George with his favorite brother, Edward. Tutors described George as lazy, immature, and eager to criticize others.

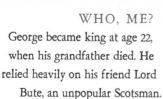

WHO, ME?
George became king at age 22, when his grandfather died. He relied heavily on his friend Lord Bute, an unpopular Scotsman.

OUT OF CONTROL
In King George's day, London was violent and wild. Here a mob protests one of George's decisions.

DADDY GEORGE
King George III and Queen Charlotte had 15 children, 13 of whom survived. George was a very strict father.

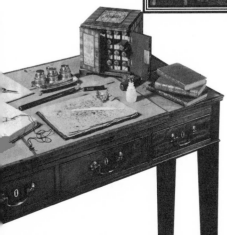

POLICY WONK
George enjoyed the business of being king. He got up early every morning and pored over paperwork at this desk.

WORLD WAR

When George became king, Britain was locked in the Seven Years' War, which involved all the powers of Europe. Here, a British army attacks the French in Canada.

STAMP OF DISAPPROVAL

After Parliament passed the Stamp Act in 1765, American colonists had to pay taxes on public and legal documents. The documents were stamped with a seal like this to show that the tax had been paid.

UNDER GEORGE'S SKIN

William Pitt was the greatest and most popular politician in England. But George thought Pitt undermined his authority.

MESSAGE IN A BOTTLE

A bottle of tea from the Boston Tea Party. After that protest, George was convinced that his American subjects must be dealt with harshly.

SHOT HEARD ROUND THE WORLD

The American Revolution began with a British victory at Lexington, Massachusetts. The battle inspired 16,000 colonists to join the rebels.

TAKE THAT!

Rebel leaders sign the Declaration of Independence, which listed their complaints against George.

"I AM INNOCENT"

The British surrender after Yorktown, the last major battle in the American Revolution. George declared himself innocent of any role in the disastrous war.

STRANGE BEDFELLOWS

In 1785, former rebel John Adams met with King George in London. Soon, the former colonies and Britain re-established ties.

FARMER GEORGE

George was obsessed with country life. The British press found this hilarious.

PLAGUED BY DOCTORS

The king's doctors bathe George in the English Channel. As he slipped into madness, his doctors tried every treatment they could imagine. It is now thought that a blood disease caused his strange symptoms.

DREAMS OF GLORY
A political cartoon shows George lecturing Napoleon, the upstart emperor of France. George vowed to fight Napoleon hand-to-hand on the battlefield.

JUBILEE
In 1809, the British people celebrated the fiftieth anniversary of George's coronation as king of Britain.

"THE LATE KING"
King George III, not long before his death. He was blind and senile, and his son Prince George had assumed power.

PART 3

A Troubled Mind

CHAPTER 14

A Brooding King

George falls victim to
A MYSTERIOUS DISEASE.

IN 1785, TWO YEARS AFTER HE WAS FORCED
to let America go, King George received a visit
from the first U.S. ambassador to Great Britain. The
ambassador was John Adams, who impressed the king
as "very proper" and respectful. "I will be free with
you," George told Adams. "I was the last to consent
to the separation, but the separation having been
made ... I have always said ... that I would be the first
to meet the friendship of the United States as an
independent power."

U.S. AMBASSADOR JOHN ADAMS presents himself to King George III. The former enemies managed to create an alliance.

George suggested that the United States should ally itself with Britain instead of France. Adams disliked the French, and the king brought the subject up with a laugh. "There is an opinion among some people," George said, "that you are not the most attached of all your countrymen to the manners of France."

"I must vow to your majesty," Adams said, "I have no attachment but to my own country."

"An honest man will never have any other," George replied. Then he bowed to end the meeting.

With that discussion, George began a friendship between Britain and the nation he had fought so bitterly to destroy. Looking back, the war seemed almost unnecessary. Despite the loss of its American colonies, the British Empire had not fallen apart. Trade with the United States was now enriching Great Britain, while the colonies had been a drain on the treasury. The Royal Navy still ruled the seas, protecting the British hold on India, Canada, and the Caribbean.

Meanwhile, the British economy was booming. The steam engine made it possible to produce goods more cheaply than ever before. Factories churned out more products with less labor. New inventions turned British textiles into the best in the world.

But the king had trouble enjoying the good health of his empire. He fell into long depressions. One night in 1788, at the age of 50, he awoke from a terrible dream. He was racked with anxiety and stomach pains.

George had been ill before. He suffered from insomnia, high fevers, and weight loss. Doctors of the time thought a person's health depended on four substances, or "humors"—black bile, yellow bile, phlegm, and blood. They bled the king in an attempt to bring these humors back into balance.

Whatever the cause of his illness, George grew terribly sick. He felt nervous and could not calm himself. Visitors to Windsor Castle, 20 miles outside of London, began to worry. Royal doctors advised the king to "take the waters" in nearby Cheltenham. He did so, drinking quarts of the sulfurous water that bubbled up from the springs in the public gardens there. He began to feel a bit better. The water, he said, gave him "a good appetite for mutton."

But the king soon began to behave oddly in public. He bustled about town with the queen on his arm, stopping to chat with each and every passerby. He spent

MUSICIANS PLAY AS GEORGE is bathed in Weymouth, his favorite summer retreat. The increasingly ill king was suffering at the hands of his doctors, who drained his blood, blistered his skin, and drugged him with opium.

entire afternoons talking excitedly about pigs with local farmers. He began to get up earlier and earlier in the morning. Once, he woke the dean of a nearby seminary before dawn and insisted on a tour of the cathedral.

When George returned to Windsor, he suffered another terrible bout of stomach pains. Then he got cramps in his legs and ugly rashes on his arms. Doctors were helpless to diagnose the problem. A few guessed it might be a form of gout. One doctor believed the king had gotten sick from sleeping in wet socks after a nighttime walk in the garden.

George's symptoms grew worse. His eyes bulged horribly and turned yellow. His urine came out purple. The veins stood out on his neck. He flew into rages or talked ceaselessly until his voice grew hoarse. The queen, he announced, had been kidnapped. A flood would soon destroy London. The king of Prussia had arrived and had demanded to speak with him. He spoke to trees and angels. He called for his horse and rode off at top speed directly into a church. "I am nervous," he repeated again and again. "I am not ill, but I am nervous."

Royal physicians tried everything they could think of. They forced George to guzzle castor oil to cleanse his system. They dosed him with laudanum, a tranquilizer made with opium. They bled him and spread chemicals on his back to raise blisters and draw pus from his body.

They considered putting hot plasters on the soles of his feet and leeches on his head. When the king could not hold still, doctors wrapped him in fine linen so he couldn't move his arms or legs.

Understandably, the patient had trouble sitting still for his treatments. The king wept and wailed and cursed the medical profession. Occasionally he grew violent. When his son George came to visit, the king grabbed him by the collar and tried to smash his head against the wall. The prince almost fainted with horror.

It had became clear to many observers that the king was no longer fit to rule. Parliament met in November 1788, but George could not deliver the customary "Speech From the Throne." With Prince George urging them on, Members of Parliament began to debate the Regency Bill, which would allow the prince to rule as regent until his father recovered from his illness.

Finally, a man named Francis Willis took over the king's treatment. Willis was a former minister with no medical training. But he had successfully treated many mentally ill people on a farm he operated in the English countryside. Willis believed the king's misbehavior was caused by moral weakness. What the king needed, he said, was discipline.

Willis kept George from seeing the queen and other members of his family. If the king talked too much or cursed, Willis tied him to a special chair. The king came to call it his "throne." Gradually, after four months of such treatment, George's symptoms began to fade. He was allowed to shave himself and spend time with the queen. Members of the royal household were greatly moved to see him kissing his wife's hands and weeping for joy at the sight of her.

With Parliament on the verge of passing the Regency Bill, George returned to his throne. The English people celebrated his return. George moved cautiously back into his old life. For now, he was king once again. He had found renewed peace of mind. But new troubles overseas would soon test his sanity.

DIAGNOSING THE KING

GEORGE III WAS TREATED BY THE BEST doctors in London—but they had no idea what was wrong with him. With a little help from modern medicine, historians finally have a diagnosis, almost two centuries after the king's death. Apparently, George suffered from porphyria, an inherited blood disease. Porphyria can cause seizures, hallucinations, and extreme anxiety. It also turns the patient's urine purple.

Today drugs can treat, but not cure, the problem. In George's time, doctors could only get out their leeches and hope for the best. It didn't help that strict rules kept them from examining the king the way they might have liked. George believed that no one should touch "the royal body" without good reason.

GEORGE'S BULGING EYES
suggest he may have had
porphyria, a blood disease.

CHAPTER 15

Revolution Again

Does the world still NEED KINGS?

KING GEORGE REGAINED HIS HEALTH in time to watch one of his great fears come true. He had often worried that the success of the American Revolution would inspire other rebellions around the world. In 1789, French revolutionaries took courage from their American counterparts and rose up against their own king. Three years later, King Louis XVI was marched to a guillotine and beheaded before a cheering mob. No doubt every king in the world shuddered and touched his own neck at the thought.

In 1799, a young general named Napoleon Bonaparte took control of France and made war with the rest of Europe. His powerful armies threatened to bring an end to monarchies across the continent.

George insisted that Napoleon be stopped. France, he had once declared, was a "savage" and "unprincipled" nation. Britain would have to go to war again. This time, George may well have felt he was fighting to save his own neck.

But in February 1801, to the horror of his friends and family, the king suffered a relapse. His stomach cramps returned. "I do feel myself very ill," George said. "I am much weaker than I was, and I have prayed to God all night that I might die, or that He would spare my reason."

Once again, Francis Willis arrived and went to work. Willis and his son punished George and lectured him on his moral failings. George raged and spat at them.

NAPOLEON, EMPEROR OF FRANCE, threatened to invade Britain—and George was eager for a fight. This British cartoon mocks George as a valiant knight striking down the dragon Napoleon.

With the approval of the queen and his own cabinet, George was held against his will in a small, cold room. Willis refused to let him see his family.

George, however, continued to conduct royal business. He read letters and signed documents. Finally one morning, the king refused to read or sign another document until he saw his family. Willis gave in. The king was joyfully reunited with his wife and daughters.

In 1803, Napoleon Bonaparte was on the march again. This time it looked as though the French commander was about to invade Britain. The threat breathed life into King George. "I should like to fight [Bonaparte] single-handed," he announced. Should the French soldiers land on British shores, he would mount a horse and lead his troops to meet them.

However, George never got a chance to make good on his boast. Napoleon turned his attention to Austria and Russia. Then, in 1805, the mighty British navy snuffed out any threat of an invasion by destroying a French fleet at the Battle of Trafalgar.

DEFENDING THE FAITH

TO GEORGE'S HORROR, THE REVOLUTIONARY spirit of the United States and France spread to Ireland, less than 100 miles off the coast of England. English Protestants lorded over an Irish population that was 90 percent Catholic. By law, Catholics could not hold government jobs, build churches, or inherit property.

In 1798, tens of thousands of Irish rose up against the English. A British army led by Lord Cornwallis crushed the rebellion.

In 1800, Parliament passed the Act of Union, merging Ireland into the British Empire. After the union, many people, including Prime Minister Pitt, pushed for the repeal of the anti-Catholic laws. But as king, George had taken an oath to protect the Protestant faith. He vowed to never allow Catholics to gain equal rights.

THE BRITISH CRUSHED the Irish Rebellion of 1798.

Unbearable Grief

GEORGE LOSES A DAUGHTER,
and finally, his life.

Even as George III sank slowly into illness and old age, his popularity continued to rise. The king's call for simple virtues seemed like a welcome relief from the war-torn world that surrounded Britain. Farmer George had become a beloved figure.

In 1809, Great Britain celebrated the fiftieth year of George's reign. Huge crowds gathered at Windsor Castle to cheer their 71-year-old king. He wore a blue coat and white pants. A tri-corner hat shielded his nearly blind eyes from the sun. Well-wishers thought he looked a bit like his old self. Two of his daughters led him by the arms as he stopped to speak with his subjects. Cries of "God Save the King" greeted George as he made his way through the crowds, and he raised his hat in thanks.

George's life at Windsor remained calm for some years. He spent most of his time with Queen Charlotte and their daughters. He prayed each morning, went riding, and worked a bit with the aid of a secretary. The surly, critical king had found a bit of peace.

But in 1810, George's happiness was shattered when Amelia, his youngest daughter and favorite child, was stricken with tuberculosis. She was just 27, and the king was devastated. A nurse who looked after the dying princess recalled how the king would come to her room each day for an hour. George would "hold her hand and bend over her to scan the face in which he was too blind to discern the onset of death."

When Amelia died, the king broke down. "The scenes of distress and crying every day," recalled the nurse, "were melancholy beyond description."

As George mourned the loss of his daughter, war raged on between Great Britain and France. George was barely aware of it. His mind and spirit had been broken. In 1811, he signed a Regency Bill allowing his son, Prince George, to take over the throne. By this time, the prince had come to respect and honor his father.

In 1815, George seemed unaffected by news that British and Prussian forces had crushed Napoleon outside Waterloo, a small village in Belgium. After the terrible fighting, 67,000 soldiers lay dead and Napoleon was sent into exile. But George lived in a different world, one without nations or glory. He was blind, deaf, and unable to think clearly.

The once powerful king drifted through the halls of Windsor in a velvet cap and purple coat. Terribly thin, wearing a long white beard, George spoke regularly to an angel he called Amelia. He saw disaster around every corner. God, he insisted, was about to flood the world, just as in Biblical times.

At times, George seemed cheerful. Other times he was filled with terror. He began referring to himself as "the late king" and no longer believed he was married to the queen. As he grew old, he spent much of his time alone, playing a harpsichord and singing loudly. When the queen died in 1818, he was too ill to understand.

In January 1820, George ceased to eat and grew ever weaker. He died that month at the age of 81. The 30,000 mourners who came to Windsor Castle heard muffled drums and trumpets along with the toll of chapel bells. They marched by torchlight from Windsor to a chapel nearby. Following eloquent words by assembled dignitaries, George's coffin was lowered into a vault. His troubles were finally over.

KING GEORGE III died in 1820, at the age of 81. He had spent almost 60 years as king.

Wicked?

Almost two centuries after King George III's death, the American Declaration of Independence survives as one of the most famous documents in history. It launched the world's first successful revolution against monarchy and planted the seeds of democracy around the globe. Sadly for the king, he played a starring role in the drama—as the villain. The Declaration declared him a "tyrant," and the label has stuck with him through the years.

Was George really a tyrant? For decades, English kings had been sharing power formally with Parliament, many of whose members were elected by the people. George was no different. He fought with Members of Parliament to retain the privileges of a king. But he accepted the fact that he had to share power.

When it came to the American colonists, George had more tolerance than he is often given credit for. Twice he accepted the repeal of tax laws when the Americans protested. When the time came to fight, he entered the war reluctantly. There were plenty of people in Parliament who called for harsher measures than their king. He also felt a responsibility to the colonists who wanted to remain loyal to the British crown.

Once the war had begun, however, the king showed his weaknesses. Many of the people who knew George III described him as stubborn and self-righteous. Convinced that he had right on his side, he often refused to hear advice from people who disagreed with him. He had several opportunities to compromise with the American rebels, and he rejected them all. Thanks in part to his stubbornness, the war dragged on for eight years and killed more than 50,000 people.

Timeline of Terror

1738

1738: George is born.

1751: George's father, Frederick, dies suddenly.

1756: The Seven Years' War begins in Europe.

1760: After the death of George II, George III becomes king of Great Britain.

1763: The Treaty of Paris ends fighting between Great Britain and France in the Seven Years' War.

1764: Parliament passes the Sugar Act, which taxes molasses in the American colonies.

1765: Parliament passes the Stamp Act, a tax on official documents.

1767: Parliament passes the Townshend Acts, taxing many household goods in the colonies.

1768: Additional British soldiers are sent to Boston to restore order.

1770: British troops fire into a threatening crowd in what comes to be called the "Boston Massacre."

1773: The Sons of Liberty conduct the "Boston Tea Party" to protest the tax on tea.

1774: The First Continental Congress meets in Philadelphia. Representatives from 12 colonies agree to band together against Britain.

1775: The American Revolution begins with a battle in Lexington, Massachusett

1776: The Declaration of Independence is written and signed in Philadelphia.

1778: American rebels sign an alliance with France.

1781: British General Cornwallis surrenders at Yorktown, Virginia.

1788: George III suffers a serious illness that affects his sanit

1799: Napoleon takes power in France; threatens to overthrow monarchies throughout Europe.

1815: Napoleon is defeated at Waterloo, Belgium.

1820: George III dies.

1820

GLOSSARY

abhor (ab-HOR) *verb* to hate someone or something

alliance (uh-LYE-uhnss) *noun* an agreement to work together

armory (AR-mur-ee) *noun* a place where weapons are stored or soldiers are trained

baptize (BAP-tize) *verb* to sprinkle water on someone's head or immerse someone in water as a symbol of acceptance into the Christian church

bayonet (BAY-uh-net) *noun* a long knife fastened to the end of a musket

cabinet (KAB-in-it) *noun* a group of advisers to the head of a government

corrupt (kuh-RUHPT) *adjective* using public office for private gain

defeatist (di-FEET-ist) *noun* someone who expects failure

despotism (DES-puh-tiz-im) *noun* the exercise of absolute power, especially in a cruel and oppressive way

diligent (DIL-uh-juhnt) *adjective* careful and hardworking

effigy (EF-ih-jee) *noun* a roughly made model of a person, made to be damaged or destroyed as a protest

empire (EM-pire) *noun* a group of countries or regions that have the same ruler

envoy (ON-voy) *noun* a person appointed to represent one government in its dealings with another

foundry (FOUN-dree) *noun* a factory for melting and shaping metal

gout (GOWT) *noun* disease in which the build up of uric acid in the blood causes swollen, painful joints

indignant (in-DIG-nuhnt) *adjective* upset out of a sense of unfairness

legislature (LEJ-iss lay-chur) *noun* a group of people who have the power to make or change laws for a country or state

123

martial law (MAR-shuhl LAW) *noun* rule by the army in a time of war, disaster, or public unrest

mercenaries (MUR-suh-ner-eez) *noun* soldiers who are paid to fight for a foreign army

musket (MUHSS-kit) *noun* a slow-loading gun with a long barrel that was used before the rifle was invented

nobility (noh-BIL-ih-tee) *noun* the people in a country or state who have been born into wealthy families and have the highest social rank

opium (OH-pee-um) *noun* an addictive drug that comes from the dried juice of the opium poppy

Parliament (PAR-luh-muhnt) *noun* the top legislature in Great Britain

pending (PEN-ding) *adjective* awaiting decision or about to happen

pious (PY-uhs) *adjective* deeply religious

plasters (PLASS-turs) *noun* during King George's time, a mustard paste placed on a person's skin as a healing treatment

porphyria (por-FIHR-ee-uh) *noun* a rare blood disease that causes dark urine, mental disturbances, and sensitivity to light

Protestant (PROT-uh-stuhnt) *noun* a Christian who does not belong to the Roman Catholic Church or Orthodox Church

revelers (REV-uhl-urz) *noun* people who engage in lively and noisy festivities

revolt (ri-VOHLT) *noun* a rebellion against a government or authority

righteous (RYE-chuhss) *adjective* morally right or virtuous

skirmish (SKUR-mish) *noun* a minor battle

tyrant (TYE-ruhnt) *noun* someone who rules others in a cruel or illegal way

Here are some books and websites with more information about King George III and his times.

BOOKS

Blashfield, Jean F. **England (Enchantment of the World, Second Series)**. New York: Children's Press, 2007. (144 pages) *Covers the history, geography, culture, and people of England.*

Ingram, Scott. **King George III**. San Diego: Blackbirch Press, 2004. (104 pages) *A well-organized and nicely illustrated look at the life of King George III.*

Schanzer, Rosalyn. **George vs. George: The American Revolution as Seen from Both Sides**. Washington, D.C.: National Geographic, 2004. (60 pages) *Explores how the lives of King George and George Washington were affected by the progress and outcome of the American Revolution.*

Sheinkin, Steve. **King George: What Was His Problem? Everything Your Schoolbooks Didn't Tell You About the American Revolution**. New York: Roaring Book Press, 2008. (208 pages) *This engaging, humorous, and informative book is illustrated with cartoons and includes fascinating, little-known facts about the American Revolution.*

WEBSITES

http://news.bbc.co.uk/2/hi/health/3889903.stm
A BBC online article on the likely cause of King George's "madness."

http://www.bbc.co.uk/history/historic_figures/george_iii_king.shtml
BBC History's profile of King George III includes links to sites with a wealth of information on George, British history, and the American Revolution.

http://www.hrp.org.uk
This site, Historic Royal Palaces, is an online tour of many of the famous buildings where British royal history took place, including Hampton Court, one of King George III's residences.

http://www.royal.gov.uk/output/Page1.asp
The official website of the British monarchy includes a profile of King George III.

For Grolier subscribers:
http://go.grolier.com/ searches: George III, King of England, Scotland, and Ireland; Washington, George; American Revolution

INDEX

Act of Union, 115

Adams, John, 77, 97, 102–104

Adams, Samuel, 52, 56, 74

Amelia, Princess, 117–118

American Revolution
beginning of, 74–76, 97, 122
major battles of, 85

Augusta, Princess, 16–17, 22, 23, 27, 39, 41, 94

Battle of Bunker Hill, 76

Battle of Lexington, 74–75, 97

Battle of Trafalgar, 114

Bonaparte, Napoleon, 99, 112–114, 118, 122

Boston Massacre, 63–64, 122

Boston Tea Party, 69–71, 97, 122

Burgoyne, General John, 82–83

Bute, Lord
as adviser to George III, 25, 26, 28, 29, 33–34, 94
as prime minister, 38
as secretary of state, 35
as tutor to George III, 23

cartoons, political, 45, 98, 99, 113

Charlotte, Queen, 42–43, 47, 68–69, 95, 117, 119

colonies, Europe's struggle for control of, 20

Continental Army, 80–82, 86

Cornwallis, General Charles, 81–82, 90, 91, 115, 122

Declaration of Independence, 12, 78, 97, 120, 122

Declaratory Act, 59–60

Dickinson, John, 76

Edward, Prince, 23, 94

First Continental Congress, 72, 122

France
as American ally, 87, 122
as enemy of England, 31–34

Frederick, Prince of Wales, 17, 18, 19, 21, 94, 122

French Revolution, 111–114

Gage, General Thomas, 63, 71, 73–76

George, Prince of Wales, 108, 118

George II, King, 17, 18–19, 21–22, 27, 31, 94, 122

George III, King
accomplishments, 39
assessment of, 120–121
birth, 16–17, 122
childhood, 19, 21–22
coronation, 28, 94, 122
daily routine, 43–44, 95
death, 99, 119, 122
death of daughter, 117–118
education, 17–18
family life, 43, 47, 67–69, 95, 117–118
fiftieth anniversary of coronation, 99, 116–117
illness, 55, 98, 105–109, 112, 114, 122
interest in country life, 44–45, 98
marriage, 42
political cartoons about, 45, 98, 99, 113

present-day diagnosis of
    illness, 110
renewal of friendly
    relations with
    America, 102–104
Grenville, George, 51, 52,
    54–55

Hancock, John, 62, 74
Henry, Patrick, 52–54
Howe, General William,
    82, 86

Irish Rebellion, 115

Jefferson, Thomas, 77
Johnson, Samuel, 71

Lafayette, General, 87
London, violence in, 40, 95

martial law, mandate of in
    Massachusetts, 71

North, Lord, 65–66, 90, 91

Olive Branch Petition, 77
Otis, James, 52, 56

Pitt, William
    death of, 88
    as leader of Whigs,
    28–29

popularity of, 33, 35,
    37, 96
and repeal of anti-
    Catholic laws, 115
and repeal of Stamp
    Act, 58–59
return as prime
    minister, 60
and Seven Years' War,
    30–35
sympathy for rebel
    cause, 72
Pitt, William the Younger,
    91
proclamation for
    "Encouragement of
    Piety and Virtue," 46
Proclamation Line of 1763,
    51, 85

Revere, Paul, 62, 74
Rockingham, Lord, 59, 60

Seven Years' War, 30–35,
    38, 39, 96, 122
slave trade, 93
smuggling, 51, 61, 69
Sons of Liberty, 56, 122
Spain, war with, 38
Stamp Act, 52, 56, 57, 58, 59,
    96, 122
Sugar Act, 51, 52, 122

taxation, protests of by
    colonists, 11, 52, 53,
    63, 120
Townshend Acts, 61, 65,
    122
Treaty of Paris, 38, 122

Valley Forge, 86, 87

Washington, General
    George, 80–81, 83,
    86–87, 90, 91
Whigs, 24–25, 55

Yorktown, British
    surrender at, 90, 97

Author's Note and Bibliography

Many of George's problems resulted because he could not get along with anyone who disagreed with him. He did not like most people. And he hated politicians because he was no good at politics, an art of compromise and personal connection. As I researched George's story, it was fun to imagine the fussy king growing red-faced and blustering at his various prime ministers.

It seems to me that a king more skilled in politics would have sailed to America—perhaps after the repeal of the Stamp Act, when his popularity was high. He would have met with men like Thomas Jefferson and Benjamin Franklin and chatted over tea. They were, after all, fellow Englishmen. Perhaps a different sort of man would have made a deal with his American friends instead of sending in troops.

Several sources were invaluable to me in writing this book:

Black, Jeremy. **George III: America's Last King**. New Haven, CT: London: Yale University Press, 2006.

Hibbert, Christopher. **George III: A Personal History**. New York: Basic Books, 1998.

Lloyd, Alan. **The King Who Lost America: A Portrait of the Life and Times of George III**. Garden City, New York: Doubleday, 1971.

—Philip Brooks